GW00650206

LAKE DISTRICT MOUNTAIN LANDSCAPE

First published in 2010 by Frances Lincoln Limited.
This second edition first published in 2015 by **Vertebrate Publishing**.
Reprinted in 2017 and 2021.

Vertebrate Publishing
Omega Court, 352 Cemetery Road, Sheffield S11 8FT, United Kingdom

Copyright © Alastair Lee 2010.
The author has asserted his right under the Copyright, Designs and Patents Act 1988
to be identified as author of this work.

A CIP catalogue record for this book is available from the British Library.

ISBN: 978-1-910240-18-2 (Hardback)
10 9 8 7 6 5 4 3

All rights reserved. No part of this work covered by the copyright herein may be reproduced or used
in any form or by any means – graphic, electronic, or mechanised, including photocopying, recording,
taping or information storage and retrieval systems – without the written permission of the publisher.

Original design by Alastair Lee – www.posingproductions.com
Production of this second edition by Nathan Ryder, Vertebrate Publishing – www.v-publishing.co.uk
Hidden Landscape text by Colin Wells. Additional text, editing and proofreading by Colin Wells.
Peaks in Sketch by David Halsted.

Printed in China on behalf of Latitude Press Ltd.

CONTENTS

TITLE PAGE: Shafts of light spot the Old Man of Coniston and Crinkle Crags.
THIS PAGE: Burning mountains of Great Gable and Kirk Fell over Innominate Tarn, Haystacks.
OVERLEAF: England's highest point, Scafell Pike, engulfed by a snow storm.

Acknowledgements

Special thanks to everybody that has made this book possible! In no particular order: Dave Birkett, Bill Birkett, Colin Wells, Stephen Reid, Mark Januszewski, Claire Wiggins, Heidi Coppock, Kirby Beard, Gaz Howell, David Halsted, Mark Edwards, The Fell and Rock Climbing Club, Richard and Jayne Davies of Dysons Arts, Anthony and Catherine Carysforth, Mum and Dad, all at Frances Lincoln Publishers, Tristan Johnson, Valerie Le Clerc and Simon Lee.

The photography featured in this book is available as Alastair Lee limited and open edition prints from www.alastairleephotography.co.uk

By the same author:
Eyes Up – Posing Productions (2002)
Forgotten Landscape – Posing Productions (2004)
Pendle, Landscape of History and Home – Frances Lincoln (2009)
Baffin Island – Frances Lincoln (2009)

THIS PAGE: The sun sets over a cloud torn Lakeland mountain scene, from Helvellyn.
OVERLEAF: Looking west from Bowfell's summit across the wild Upper Esk Valley.
PAGE 10: A snow-capped Kirkfell, Scafell Pike and Bowfell as seen from Birker Fell; Windtorn ice plasters the rocks on Scafell.

P e r s p e c t i v e s

New Perspectives

This book focuses on the high mountains of Lakeland – a domain filled with many scenic treasures and adventures for those who are prepared to put in the effort to reach it. For the majority of visitors, it remains an undiscovered country, and I admit that I used to be one of them. Like perhaps many first-time tourists encountering Lakeland in peak season, my overwhelming sensation was one of disillusionment. The roads and dales were crowded and congested, while an air of tweeness seemed to dominate many of the quaint towns and villages I passed through. After enduring a night in a wet and noisy Langdale campsite I found myself becalmed behind a dawdling campervan puttering uncertainly over Wrynose Pass. It was hardly the great outdoors experience I had imagined. There seemed to be little the young adventurer might relate to. From this low point there was only one place to go: up – literally. And thanks to this, a revelation occurred. I came to appreciate how simple it was to escape the honey pots and find solitude in the mountains. Just a few minutes stroll away from a car park was often all that was required, while a half-hour or more brought me the freshness and challenge of ever-changing upland terrain that I craved. Here, it seemed to me, was where the real Lakeland lay. But, as a photographer, something that was more difficult to ignore was the seemingly endless racks of clichéd picture postcards in every shop in the district. It struck me that the plethora of Lakeland artwork, paintings, photography and calendars on display were all remarkably similar. Indeed it seemed surprising to me that some well photographed scenes (such as Wastwater – 'Britain's Favourite View', according to ITV and *Coronation Street's* very own Sally Whittaker) didn't suffer from photographic erosion due to the thousands and thousands of shots taken there! But this romanticised ideal of tranquility certainly isn't the only attraction the landscape of the Lake District has to offer.

As a consequence, lakeside images are sparse in this book; its title is unambiguous: *Mountain Landscape*. It's about the mountains themselves, their history, geology, ecology and culture you find in and on them – and my experiences trying to capture their essence on film. To do this effectively unavoidably means one thing: taking to the hills. As a result I have hiked all over the high land of the Lake District with the intention of portraying its grandeur and the exhilaration of exploring it. My constant aim was to seek unusual or dramatic light and weather in order to cut through familiar preconceptions of Lakeland's uplands and to accentuate their raw wildness. These 'snapshots in time' have been made permanent through the photographic process and for me they are therefore incredibly strong and vibrant personal memories I can return to again and again. With this book, now they are memories that can be shared with others.

Previous Spread: Not quite the sunrise shot I originally had in mind. I shivered in a white-out for about an hour at the top of Hardknott Pass hoping 'something' would happen. It did. A brief break in the clouds allowed a dramatic counterpoint between the storm-ravaged sky and alpenglow-tinted snow.

Left: Sunset from Kentmere Pike. Above: Spindrift racing down the slopes of Kentmere Pike, Ill Bell provides the backdrop; mini-Andean snow flutings on Kentmere Pike.

Scafell Pike reveals itself after a winter storm in a 360-degree panorama from Bowfell's summit. Everywhere I looked something was happening, as if I was surrounded by a fast-moving laser light show. Dramatic shafts of light, a highly mobile sky, cloud bursts and some snow cover; nature can be such a show off! Standing alone in bitter temperatures in awe of one's surroundings is an experience that never really leaves you. For the next few days it seemed as if part of me remained in a trance, bewitched, still on the mountain. This feeling of visiting another world is what draws me to the summits. When I shut my eyes I'm still there. (Sketch of this image on pages 166–7.)

The much-photographed view of Wasdale Head over Wastwater with the famous peaks of Yewbarrow, Great Gable and Scafell Pike. (This is typical of the type of shot you won't find in this book.)

The Langdale Pikes photographed from 'that layby'; it's surprising that nobody's set up a photo booth there. Below is the classic view of Derwent Water and the Northern Fells, taken from the Castle Hill viewpoint. Like many well-photographed scenes it's a matter of minutes from the car.

A less familiar view of England's highest peak, Scafell Pike, with the magnificent East and Esk buttresses in view. Viewed from the western slopes of Crinkle Crags.

A magnificent cloud inversion floods the Langdale Valley from Pike o'Blisco. Skiddaw, Helvellyn and Fairfield frame the horizon beyond Pike o'Stickle and Harrison Stickle. Side Pike is just poking out of the clouds on the bottom right. (Sketch of this image on page 175.)

The effects of altitude

Once you have reached a certain height, taking good photographs is, in many ways, easy. Things happen up there that you'd never experience or even know about down in the valley. There's nothing more exciting than arriving in thick cloud, knowing that it's a temperature inversion and that you are going to rise above it all to witness a spectacular cloud base below your feet and the peaks forming islands in a sea.

Light behaves differently up high; everything seems sharper, although this effect can easily be reversed if the cloud base is low. I love the ethereal quality of light immediately pre- and post-sunrise in the uplands, where it remains much brighter than in the valleys. The physical exertion required to gain a high vantage point also heightens perception; endorphins and adrenaline produced by exercise combine with the thrill of the summit view and create an extraordinary sense of well-being. It is perhaps an ineffable sensation, but hopefully some of it will remain ever-present in these photographs.

OPPOSITE ABOVE: Low cloud rolls down Ennerdale from the Irish Sea with High Style looming large. INSET: Sunrise from Esk Hause. Rising mist creates some interesting lighting effects. INSET LEFT: Decending Scafell Pike.

ABOVE: Misty valleys create a layered effect when viewed from above. In this case the Old Man of Coniston from the summit of Helvellyn.

Chapel Stile in the mist, Great Langdale. Admittedly, I didn't have to climb very high to capture this image, which is fortunate since it was very late on a summer's evening. I was actually travelling up to the Lakes in order to get an early start the next day rather than with the intention of taking pictures. However it neatly illustrates the fact that you do need to gain some height in order to appreciate the scene.

One of the most popular tourist attractions in Lakeland is Rydal Mount between Ambleside and Grasmere, famous for the fact that from 1813 it was home to the Lake District's most famous poet, William Wordsworth. Thousands of visitors flock here, intrigued by the reputation of the literary giant. But there is also a more 'hands on' approach to appreciating the picturesque setting that the great wordsmith immortalised: by making a short but steep climb to Nab Scar. From this vantage point the unique and seemingly crafted landscape of the Lake District is revealed in its full glory, particularly when the late season tints the landscape with autumn colours. From here the view stretches from Lake Windermere, Coniston and Langdale to the distinctive lump of Loughrigg Fell and Rydal Water.

LEFT: The author takes in the view from Nab Scar above Rydal Water.

While descending Helvellyn as the evening light was fading, an almost full moon rose dramatically. This gave me the idea of coming back to take some photographs by its crepuscular light. I thought frozen water might help reflect some of the moon's glimmer, so I headed for Red Tarn below Helvellyn. It was pitch black when I arrived and bitterly cold, with a strong north wind, so I headed up to Striding Edge seeking shelter on its lee side. Apart from the cold, I needed to be out of the wind in order to steady the camera during the long exposures required. I was out for about six hours and it was one of the most spiritually uplifting – and simultaneously spooky – experiences I've had in the Lakeland fells. This shot is taken from Striding Edge looking towards an unreal Nethermost Pike and Dollywaggon Pike frozen into an arctic moonscape. In great contrast, the west coast neon strip of Morecambe and Blackpool intrudes on the horizon, a reminder that the illusion of wilderness in the Lake District is fragile and easily broken.

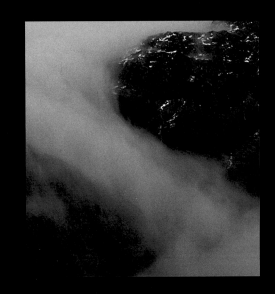

Hidden Landscape

Scars, mines and mysteries

Hidden Landscape

What explains the attraction of England's Lake District? What is it about a mountain range that ranks as a minnow on a world scale that seduces so many of its visitors? Part of the explanation may lie in its sense of timelessness. This is an ancient landscape hewn from a myriad of natural and human events. Whereas jagged Alpine terrain can appear raw, even brash and unfinished, the Lakeland Fells might be regarded as the equivalent of a sculpture that has been worked on for many years by a craftsman. As a consequence, much of the fells' subtle beauty derives from their softer, more intimate, human scale, compared to higher mountains.

The reason for this lies in the fact that the fells are much, much older than their soaring European, American or Asian counterparts. The ancient volcanic and sedimentary rocks that form the heart of the district are the worn-down stubs of a mighty Himalaya-sized chain that existed half a billion years ago. Orchestrating the forces of wind, water, ice and vegetation, the changing climate has been a sculptor spending millions of years perfecting its work. And over the last 5,000 years, people have taken over and accelerated the task. This combination of elements has lent a unique form and quality to Lakeland. As a consequence, it is one of the most distinctive and clearly recognisable landscapes in the world.

The results of such a complex genesis may be admired in the blink of an eye, but deciphering the code behind the landscape is much more difficult. Many of Lakeland's most famous views are the result of seemingly improbable events. Tranquil crags and screes turn out to be ancient quarries and industrial spoil heaps; broad, tundra-like ridges framing the skyline are the result of millennia of sheep grazing; vast heathery moorlands forming the central fells' skirtlands prove to be the abandoned fields from long-forgotten prehistoric farming attempts. Everywhere one looks in Lakeland, there is nearly always a hidden meaning behind the 'natural' beauty.

PREVIOUS SPREAD: The northern fells swamped in a cloud inversion, as seen from Pillar.

RIGHT FROM THE TOP: Ancient 'in-bye' grazings at Wasdale; Dry stone walls lead to the Langdale Pikes; Water pools near Elterwater; Medieval field boundaries at Wasdale Head. OPPOSITE: Coniston Water and the Coniston Old Man, as seen descending Wetherlam.

Wherever you look there is a hidden story beneath the landscape's modern patina. Coniston Old Man is a strange name for the outstanding peak of south-western Lakeland, but scrape a bit and you find a meaning. 'Man' is probably a corruption of an original Celtic word 'maen' – 'stone', which in turn passed into regional dialect as a term meaning a large cairn of stones, of which the mountain summit sports a prime example. The Celtic origins of the mountain's name emphasise how much this is an ancient landscape shaped by ancient activity. Between about 1000–1500 BC the densely wooded uplands around peripheral mountains such as the Old Man saw a dramatic forest clearance as a Bronze Age population explosion spilled on to higher ground, aided by a less wet and slightly warmer climate than today. Dry stone walls were built around fields with the stones picked from the newly won soils and small stone circles were erected. But the breaking of the wildwood started an ecological time-bomb ticking as the settlers' ploughs began to exhaust thin upland soils. When the climate shifted to a cooler, wetter regime around 800 BC, the land was abandoned as rapidly as it had been occupied and peaty moorland reclaimed the land for nature. The fell slopes between 200–300 metres (such as those seen in the above picture descending below the steeper slopes of the mountain stretching towards Coniston Water) were left littered with a redundant infrastructure of field boundaries and cairns, now hidden by rank heather, mat-grass and rushes. This poignant landscape was later further scarred when quarrymen and copper miners began to hew the very mountain fabric itself in the eighteenth century, an activity still continuing to this day. When viewing the scarcely healed quarrying wounds and exhausted soils of the moors below, the words of singer Josh Ritter seem especially resonant: 'The land is too changed to ever change'.

Above: The 'Priest Hole' Cave, Dove Crag, Dovedale.

The history behind the 'Priest Hole' remains a mystery. It is probably a natural cavity which has been modified by generations of hill users for use as a shelter, akin to a Scottish 'howff'. In the past it is likely that shepherds utilised it (the remains of ancient sheep-folds scatter the hillslopes below) but today you are more likely to encounter adventurous walkers and climbers in search of a bivouac. 'Priest Hole' is likely to be simply a nickname, a reference to the famous hiding places favoured by Catholic recusants in ancient houses during times of persecution. Nevertheless, despite the lack of solid evidence, a feature as unusual as this has naturally garnered many myths. Some theorise that the cave has a more colourful past connected to prehistoric miners, smugglers or genuine religious persecution. The only certainty is that the enigma of the hole will continue to fascinate those who pass by.

It is difficult at first sight to believe that the alpine arena of Great Langdale effectively represents one of Britain's first industrial landscapes. A huge chute of scree that drops from the summit of Pike o'Stickle is in fact littered with the waste from stone axe manufacture. But there is much more than just time-softened debris remaining from this distant hive of activity; much of the present-day landscape owes its very appearance to this ancient industry, resulting in what the archaeologist Richard Bradley has described as, 'one of the most dramatic field monuments in Britain'.

LEFT: The Langdale Pikes as seen from Pike o'Blisco.

ABOVE: The scar of Britain's oldest industrial landscape, a 5000 BC stone axe 'factory'.

Around 3800 BC the uplands around the head of the Langdale Valley began being deforested by people. The cleared land, which became permanent, was concentrated around the mountains of Bowfell and the Langdale Pikes, which were beginning to be developed as quarries and stone axe factories. To this day, surprising amounts of material remain, abandoned among the high crags and quarried faces. Here and there may be found balls of granite, once used to smash Langdale's volcanic tuffs into axe-sized pieces which could then be shaped into elegant, polished axe heads – the power tools of the Stone Age. Langdale became one of the most important production sites in Europe, supplying the tools with which an unparalleled onslaught on the woodlands of Britain was initiated by the earliest farmers (Langdale axes have been found all over the British Isles and as far away as central Europe). The wealth generated by this axe trade must have been considerable; there has been much conjecture over whether this might have helped to fund the origins of the many prestigious megalithic monuments to be found in and around the fringes of the Lake District.

Wealth from the hills

The Langdale axe 'factory' represents merely the beginning of the quarrying and mining industries which have been a continual feature of the Lakeland scene ever since prehistory. Nearly anywhere you travel in the district, whether it be high, expansive uplands or intimate wooded dales, you are rarely far from the evidence of attempts to dig riches from the seams of the earth.

Copper, lead and graphite were the minerals particularly prized by medieval and Elizabethan prospectors and much of the area was scoured for valuable mineral veins. Copper was being worked as early as the thirteenth century, in the Goldscope Mine in the Newlands Valley, where there were also veins of lead. In the sixteenth century technically advanced German miners were imported to Keswick to help exploit Lakeland's copper. At first there was local hostility, and the miners were forced to live in isolation on one of the islands of Derwentwater. Eventually, they became integrated into the community. The success of this is shown by the parish register of Crosthwaite Church which reveals that 176 children were born of German fathers between 1565 and 1584.

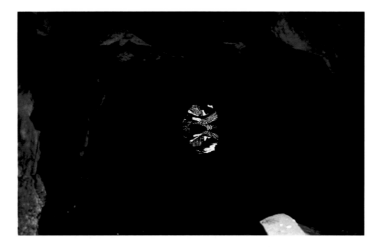

Another rare mineral for which Lakeland became famous was graphite, known locally as 'black lead', 'wad' or 'plumbago'. For a time in the eighteenth and early nineteenth century a mine at Seathwaite was a major source of a material valued for its use in the casting of bomb casings, round-shot and cannon balls, as well as the glazing of pottery, fixing of blue dyes, the marking of sheep and the manufacture of pencils at Keswick. So valuable did this commodity become that armed guards were posted at the entrance to the mine at one point. By the 1830s output was in decline and today all that remains of this once strategically vital industry are mysterious fern-shrouded holes amongst the trees on the steep slopes above Seathwaite.

After agriculture, the industry which has left the most significant legacy on the Lakeland landscape is slate quarrying, which continues to this day. The beginnings of the industry can be traced back to the late eighteenth century when a demand for roofing slate began to grow as the Industrial Revolution accelerated. Later, in the twentieth century, Lakeland slate began to be used for general building purposes as well as roofing. Although the demand for Lakeland slate and its level of exploitation is now greatly reduced, the need for slate remains, partly thanks to National Park planning rules that stipulate new buildings need to harmonise with their surroundings. The continued use of the material – and hence its extraction – is likely therefore to continue well into the future. Fortunately, despite its former size, the industry has left few of the landscape-scarring legacies that disfigure parts of Snowdonia. Instead, trees now shroud many of the abandoned workings, while others, such as the great Cathedral Quarry near Langdale with its 40-foot high main chamber, have become tourist attractions or venues for new outdoor recreation, such as 'sport climbing' and abseiling.

RIGHT: The impressive Cathedral Quarry, Little Langdale.

For many, Buttermere occupies the most beautiful and tranquil dale in the Lake District. Hemmed in by high mountain passes on all sides save the north, the extra effort required to gain this haven and its surrounding fells is rewarded by peaceful days on high plateau-like summits and sinuous ridges. In early summer the air above the springy turf of the broad whale-backed hills of Robinson, Grisedale Pike and Grasmoor can cascade with sky-lark song as you pick a way over 'stone stripes', 'stone nets' and 'stone circles'. These mysterious geometric patterns of small coarse rocks and finer material have been sorted by the action of winter frosts gently heaving the thin soils of the mountain plateau. They are not the only arctic tint to the landscape; the rolling high ground around Buttermere has long been an English stronghold for the dotterel or 'Mossfool': a beguilingly trusting wading bird with striking chestnut plumage and a white head-band like a smartly turned out tennis player. Dotterel are sub-arctic birds, their Lakeland mountain fastnesses represent-ing the southern extremity of their European range. Sadly, as the climate has continued to warm, so the birds seem to be becoming scarcer – as indeed has the 'patterned ground' of sorted stones which has begun to retreat upwards in the past two decades as hard frosts have become a less frequent feature of Cumbria's winters.

RIGHT: The head of Lake Buttermere flanked by Grasmere, Robinson and Fleetwith Pikes.

OVERLEAF: Despite its overwhelmingly bucolic setting, Keswick, posi-tioned picturesquely at the outflow of Derwentwater and overlooked by the burly Skiddaw and the sculpted fells of Newlands, has always been a business town. Mercantile activity, rather than agriculture, is its lifeblood. The urban area expanded in the mid-sixteenth century when a mining boom commenced with the first 'strikes' of copper then graphite. Later slate quarrying maintained prosperity. As these indus-tries declined, tourism, beginning in the late eighteenth century, replaced it as the major employer in the twentieth century. Tourism itself has now evolved, with fell-walking and other outdoor pursuits becoming predominant, helping to explain why today, in a town of only around 4,000 inhabitants, there are almost two dozen shops specialis-ing in selling outdoor equipment. (Sketch of image on page 173.)

Today, the western fells are among the most remote and least frequented of the Lakeland summits thanks to their comparative inaccessibility by car. 125 years ago the situation was, if anything, reversed. The western fells were a popular destination while now-busy central dales such as Langdale (which was the last place in Cumbria to receive a mains electricity supply in 1960) remained comparatively quiet. The reason was partly to do with the rail network, established by the mid-nineteenth century, which served the thriving Victorian industrial centres of the west Cumberland coast but which terminated in the east at Windermere. The other attraction was the high mountain crags in this area.

The first generation of technical rock climbers, appearing from the 1870s onwards, may have been motivated by the sporting challenge of a route as opposed to merely gaining a summit, but they were still mountaineers at heart. Pillar Rock, the most alpine of all Lakeland summits (and the only one which requires rock climbing to reach it) became a magnet for these early pioneers.

LEFT: The spectacular Pillar Rock on a winter's evening.

ABOVE: The daunting prospect of Pillar Rock, as seen via the standard approach from Ennerdale.

180-degree view of Great Langdale, as seen from Side Pike at first light.
(Sketch of this image on page 174.)

The snowline in this photograph probably approximates to the upper limit of dense forest that occupied the Langdale Valley before the first farming communities arrived 5,000 years ago. Lighter birch, aspen and willow scrub on the higher ridges and cols were first cleared by the Neolithic stone axe manufacturers but the valley bottom with its thicker soil remained as largely impenetrable forest until around 3,000 years ago. The present day dry stone walled fields, although known to exist from at least the medieval period, probably have their origins in this older, Bronze Age reclamation.

ABOVE: Golden light strikes the side of Blea Rigg; Frosty leaves underfoot, Great Langdale.

Framed by Great Gable, Green Gable and Sprinkling Tarn, the wild, tundra-like uplands to the south-west of Borrowdale belie their origins as a domestic livestock raising ground over a thousand years old. In the thirteenth and fourteenth centuries this corner of Lakeland lay on the boundary between two great sheep and cattle ranches run by the powerful monastic houses of Furness and Fountains Abbeys. In many ways, these Cistercian ecclesiastical bodies behaved like modern agribusiness corporations. They were leading agents in the international wool trade of the time with fleeces exported as far afield as continental Europe. Down below in the valley, the hamlet of Grange in Borrowdale became the administrative centre from which the monks of Furness managed their central Lakeland estate holdings. Echoes from this ancient period of intensive use remain in the form of the lonely treeless landscape and some of the original ranching boundaries, one of which, constructed partly from wooden palings and preserved in peat, was excavated by archaeologists near Stockley Bridge fifteen years ago.

The head of Ennerdale, home to a lonely youth hostel, Black Sail, is one of the most wild and remote corners of the Lake District, with the only exits to the south passing over high, rough passes. Thankfully, the blanket conifer afforestation which has scarred the area since 1926 is now gradually being reduced to allow a wilder valley to develop by natural processes. Part of Ennerdale's distinctive character is provided by the jumble of hummocks and hollows at the very head of the valley. These are the huge piles of stony moraine churned and pushed by the last spasms of the final glaciers to form in western Lakeland around 11,000 years ago.

Mountain Craft

The King, the sheep and the crag

A 360-degree view from just below Helvellyn's summit. The popular Striding Edge and St Sunday Crag take centre stage. Being on the tops in late evening light can be a magical experience, just make sure you've got a head torch to get down (not that I ever have). (A sketch of this image is on page 164–5.)

PREVIOUS SPREAD: Dave Birkett on his own route *Missing*, Blea Rigg Crag, a mile or so from his house in Little Langdale; Dave Birkett abseiling from the top of Dove Crag; Stewart Hughes leads the way in this 360-degree view of Hare Crag, Eskdale.

Mountain Craft

The birthplace of rock climbing in England, the UK, and, some claim, the known universe, is often said to be Napes Needle on Great Gable. First ascended (solo) by Old Etonian Walter Parry Haskett Smith on 29 June 1886, turn-of-the-century photographers, such as the celebrated Abraham brothers consolidated the Needle's fame by photographing climbers on it and shooting the very first climbing movie there in 1911. Pictures of climbers on the Needle began appearing in periodicals and photographic shop windows as far away as London and had a powerful effect in recruiting more people to try climbing. It is therefore easy to see how the glamorous Needle became associated in the mind of the general public with a sport that was completely new to them. However, climbing had actually been taking place well before Haskett Smith's celebrated ascent. Indeed the mountains and fells of the Lake District have been scaled by people for probably at least 7,000 years while the first recognised rock climb had been achieved as long ago as 1802 when Samuel Taylor Coleridge descended Broad Stand on Scafell. By the 1870s several technical rock climbs had been undertaken in the mountains of the Lake District, most notably on Pillar Rock and Scafell.

Nevertheless, the publicity surrounding the early Victorian ascents of Napes Needle marks the beginning of the modern sport of rock climbing whose development accelerated from this date. Within a decade, a system for grading the difficulty of rock climbs had evolved which is still used to this day, while an ever-growing band of enthusiasts were succeeding on increasingly difficult climbs. The opening of the railways after the mid-nineteenth century also brought a greater number and diversity of tourists than previously seen in Lakeland. Now, the professional middle-classes as well as the leisured wealthy could make affordable regular visits. Many harboured alpine aspirations and so the craggiest fells such as Pillar, Great Gable and Scafell became popular destinations for hiking, scrambling and now rock climbing. Equipment and maps remained relatively primitive however, and knowledge of weather, 'conditions' or objective dangers was limited. Yet, such was the skill of the early climbers that no serious accident occurred until 1903.

BELOW: Practising for higher climbs on the Langdale crags on the Langdale Boulders. This form of unroped climbing on low cliffs and rocks is known as 'bouldering'. Many young climbers mistakenly think of it as a relatively modern development, but it has in fact been part of the rainbow of rock climbing styles since the beginning of the sport. (The first informal guide to a bouldering area was penned by Aleister Crowley in 1898 while the first 'official' one was published in the *Fell And Rock Climbing Club Journal* way back in 1916.)

ABOVE TOP RIGHT: An old piton removed from Blea Rigg Crag. Pitons have been in use in Britain since the 1930s to protect rock climbs and winter routes although they are rarely used in summer nowadays. ABOVE BOTTOM RIGHT: Belaying on Central Gully in winter with modern equipment.

The Lakeland fells now see unprecedented levels of popularity with a dizzying array of mountain pursuits, old and new, to choose from. Naturally, the most popular remains fell walking, but scrambling, rock climbing, winter climbing, fell-running, mountain biking, paragliding, even hound trailing, are also popular. The connection between mountain craft and community still remains; old ice axes, crampons and ropes are on display in bars of the Old Dungeon Ghyll in Langdale; the annual Borrowdale fell race adds the name of the winner every year to a plaque in the Scafell Hotel Bar while the names of the Wasdale fell race winners are to be found in the Wasdale Inn. They signify a deep-felt and long-standing empathy between the local community and athletic endeavour pursued on the fells.

ABOVE LEFT: Fell runner on the summit of Scafell Pike during the Wasdale Fell Race, July 2005. ABOVE RIGHT: Napes Needle circa 1940. Jim Birkett is on the arête (right hand skyline), Len Muscroft on ledge, Charlie Wilson climbing Wasdale Crack (the original route of ascent), lower belayer unknown. Both the *Wasdale Crack* (Charlie Wilson in situ) and *Needle Arête* (Jim Birkett leading) are now given the grade 'Hard Severe'. *Photos courtesy of Bill Birkett picture library.*

King of the Hill

The Lakeland crags attract climbers of all skill levels. Some make fleeting visits to 'tick' a few classic routes or to try a famous test piece, whilst others are more prolific at adding new routes. But when it comes to sustained cutting-edge modern climbing, none can compare to one particular local stoneworker and cragsman. Dave Birkett, a local man raised on a Langdale hill farm, is also one of the most accomplished rock climbers in the world. As a result, the Lake District is once again in the forefront of climbing advances. Here Birkett is battling a vicious overhang on his route *Nowt but a Fleein' Thing* on Cam Crag above the Wasdale Screes. The picture both captures the athletic dynamism required to ascend the hardest of modern routes, and the timeless environment in which Birkett has charted his recent campaign of extreme climbing, a quiet backwater of the Cumbrian landscape that Birkett calls 'a lost Kingdom of the Lake District'.

LEFT: Dave Birkett's stunning 2004 climb is named after the famous response given by the legendary Victorian Wasdale farmer and mountain guide Will Ritson, when asked what he thought of Scafell as a climbing ground: 'Nowt but a fleein' thing would git up theer' was his scornful retort.

RIGHT: Carved from Langdale Rhyolite, the climbers' climber and undoubted king of the hill, Dave Birkett.

The Lost Kingdom   Cam Crag, Wasdale Screes

Despite over one hundred years of pioneering by climbers in the Lake District, Dave Birkett still contrived to discover arguably the best 'line' in the area while wandering around Wastwater in 2003; a reward for his adventurous spirit. Ironically, the location is in one of the most frequented valleys in the district: Wasdale, the route to England's highest peak, Scafell Pike. Nevertheless it is worth noting that access to Cam Crag itself is pretty tough, its overhangs defended by extensive

scree slopes (some parts loose and greasy) and patches of a veritable jungle of bracken and thorn bushes, all very steep and unmarked.

LEFT: Dave Birkett on his latest addition to Cam Crag *Hasta Sin Owt Ert Hoonds?*, 2007 Wasdale. (Translation: local Cumbrian dialect for, 'I say, have you seen the hunting dogs?')

ABOVE: The Screes, Wastwater, location of the small but perfectly formed Cam Crag. Look for a shadow under an overhanging rock just right of the centre of the picture, adjacent to a thin scree slope running from the top.

Climbing on Scafell is without doubt one of the finest climbing experiences to be had in the British Isles. Apart from the opportunity to revel in the crag's great history and climb on some fantastic rock, it is the sheer sense of scale that really makes the experience stand out.

ABOVE: Scafell Pinnacle beneath the crag.

RIGHT: Colin Wells leads a classic route on Scafell Pinnacle, as seen from the 'West Wall Traverse'. Scafell Pike's summit and path from Mickledore in full view as well as Scafell Pike Crags and Great Gable further left.

'When you get to Mickledore in the springtime it's like being reborn' – Dave Birkett

Scafell is Dave's favourite place and it's easy to see why. The mountain's collection of buttresses, rock walls and pinnacles offer some of the grandest rock architecture in Lakeland. Climbs here also offer peerless views by virtue of their location on England's highest peak. Dave was born of farming stock and spent his childhood under the wing of a hill-farming grandfather with whom he helped herd sheep on the Lakeland fells. This sowed the seeds of a long and intimate relationship with the mountain landscape.

ABOVE: View of England's highest peak, Scafell Pike, from the adjoining peak Scafell on a warm summer's day. LEFT: Dave Birkett on his own route on Scafell's Deep Gill in the main crag, the aptly named *Death Arête* (E8 6c).

RIGHT: Perhaps the finest rock face in the Lakes, Central Buttress, Scafell, basking in the evening summer light. A climber on the classic *Saxon* (E2) can be spotted just up and right of the picture centre.

'The most fearsome crag in Britain' –
Jim Birkett

That was the synopsis of Scafell's East Buttress by Dave Birkett's other grandfather. Like Dave himself, grandfather Jim was a rare example of an indigenous, working class, Lakeland rock-climber, and also one of the best in the land between the wars. Like his descendent, he too created the hardest climbs in the Lake District in his time. One of the most notable was the *May Day Climb* currently accorded the grade of E1 5b (although Dave and his climbing uncle, Bill, consider it actually quite a bit harder than this). When it was first climbed in 1938 a climb of this grade was perhaps a decade and half ahead of its time. (Originally the notoriously modest Jim gave it a lowly 'Very Severe' grade.)

Partly because of this family legacy, the East Buttress has now also become a special place for Dave. You could easily describe it as Dave's 'hunting ground' since he has made the first ascents of no fewer than five exceptionally difficult routes (*Another Lonely Day*, *Welcome to the Cruel World*, *Return of the King*, *Talbot Horizon* and *New Horizons*), all of which remain unrepeated (at the time of writing in 2009).

LEFT: First light strikes the East Buttress.

RIGHT: The crag really comes to life after mid-day, once the shadows bring out all the crags features.

ABOVE FROM THE TOP: Dave Birkett on his East Buttress 'extremes'; *Talbot Horizon* (photo courtesy of Bill Birkett photo library); Hanging from a rope prior to the first ascent of *Return of the King*; Long moves on *New Horizons*.

LEFT: Another of the Lake District's famous climbing areas, Dow Crag, situated just east of the Old Man of Coniston. The route *Eliminate A,* first climbed in 1923, tackles the left-most buttress. Whilst it is not technically too difficult, the exposed positions are superb and the climb remains a classic; it is regarded as one of Britain's finest rock climbs. Scafell's East Buttress is visible peeking over the shoulder of the ridge to the right.

The Majestic Gimmer Crag

This fine, airy crag, one of the most architecturally impressive climbing arenas in the Lakeland Fells, is often surrounded by examples of its namesake: a 'gimmer' is an old northern English dialect term for a ewe between one and two years old, used more usually these days to mean one that has not yet borne a lamb. The crag itself was largely shunned by the very earliest climbers for the simple reason that it is so intimidatingly smooth and steep. But these were the very qualities that attracted the second wave of technical climbers of the 1920s who arrived on the scene armed with a bold balance climbing technique, better belaying procedures and – most importantly – new fangled rubber plimsolls to aid adhesion on the frequently flawless rock. Most of the popular and classic 'Very Severe' routes on the crag date from this surge in climbing standards.

The fabulous view of Stickle Tarn and Pavey Ark, a familiar sight for all walkers who head from Great Langdale to the tops. A short but steep approach (40 mins) is all it takes.

Above Left: Scramblers on the classic *Jack's Rake*, the easiest route on the crag (without walking around the sides).

Right: Dave Birkett on his own route, *Impact Day*, the hardest route on the crag at E8/9. It is situated on the walls of East Gully.

Overleaf: Dawn rises over Langdale in early summer. Ethereal light suffuses Blea Tarn, Crinkle Crags, Bowfell and the Langdale Pikes. The picture was taken from a vantage point halfway up Lingmoor Fell. The following page shows the same scene six months later as autumn arrives.

Superficially, the broken nature of many Lakeland outcrops does not make them automatically appealing to rock climbers. However, the ancient, weathered geology makes the rock very solid and reveals itself to be excellent for climbing.

ABOVE: Wallowbarrow Crag, Duddon Valley. Left: Stephen Reid seconds a first ascent on Pillar Rock. Despite its history and popularity, unclimbed rock still remains for those keen enough to seek out the lines.

RIGHT: A rare sheet of steep blank rock on Gillercombe Buttress high above Borrowdale. No surprises then that Dave Birkett has climbed this stunning feature resulting in *Caution*, graded E8.

OVERLEAF: The aptly named 'Haystacks'. It's easy to see why this was Alfred Wainwright's favourite location in the Lake District. The view across the edge of Innominate Tarn reveals Kirk Fell and Gable Crag on Great Gable to the left.

An early start to the day can often be rewarded by special moments in the mountains. While staying in Langdale, I awoke before sunrise to be greeted by a fairly unremarkable scene: a clear sky but not much in the way of morning mist or other conditions which might bring a bit of drama to the landscape. Nevertheless, I chanced my luck and headed north in the knowledge that twenty minutes' drive and a short walk would allow me to gain the vantage point of Catbells overlooking Derwentwater and Borrowdale. As I dropped over Dunmail Raise my heart raced – the entire valley was filled with a superb cloud inversion, like of bowl of gently simmering fog soup. I raced through the Keswick mists happy and confident I'd be climbing up above them just in time to catch first light.

FROM THE LEFT: Looking north from the Hell's Wall, Borrowdale; Looking east down Borrowdale; Mist creeping up and down Newlands Valley; Crag Hill and Robinson in the Northern Fells in view; Dead wood above Hell's Wall.

PREVIOUS SPREAD: One of the district's most impressive hills; Blencathra or Saddleback. The weather clears after an autumn storm enhancing the hill's distinctive scalloped flanks. Because of its relatively soft, slate geology, the hill is almost devoid of rock or crags except for the popular 'Sharp Edge', a moderate scramble hidden in the clouds on the right hand side.

OVERLEAF: Early morning light strikes the elephant's hide of Skiddaw and Blencathra, from Catbells.

While Dave Birkett's rock climbing feats are famous, his unique and valuable contribution to the local farming community is less well known. Sheep sometimes find themselves cragfast on exposed and dangerous ledges onto which they have climbed or fallen and cannot escape. To the rescue comes vertical sheep wrangler Dave Birkett. Dave's role as an unofficial one man 'sheep rescue team' keeps him busy after hours when his unique combination of farming and climbing expertise come into their own. Dave's climbing stories pale by comparison to his animal rescue tales – on one occasion he was asked to rescue some ferocious hunting dogs but warned that being savaged by the bloodthirsty hounds was a real risk. (As if swinging around on a rope above the abyss while wrestling with a panicking animal wasn't frightening enough!)

LEFT: Evening summer light floods the Upper Eskdale Valley, with the Scafell range providing the backdrop. The cliff just right of centre in the picture was the scene for

Valley walks are deliberately omitted from this book since they are covered so much elesewhere. The walk to Upper Eskdale via the river is so good however, it can't be ignored, plus it does take you to one of the highest valley floors in the park. The route leads you along the River Esk, along the valley to Upper Eskdale. Emerald pools, bursts of purple heather and miniature gorges carved from quartzite rock provide an ever-changing scene unlike anywhere else in the Lakes. The river rises on the south side of the Scafell range and, since this is one of the wettest places in Britain, it rarely runs dry.

ABOVE FROM LEFT: Valerie and Simon Lee enjoying the shallower waters higher up the river; Mini waterfalls with Bowfell visible in the background; Emerald pools perfect for a summer's dip; Old mining bridge heading for Upper Eskdale.

RIGHT: The spectacular River Esk in full summer bloom.

One of the most enjoyable mountain crafts pursued in the Lake District is that of scrambling. This takes place on those intermediate crags where walkers fear to tread but which climbers consider to be easy enough to dispense with a rope for protection. The relatively easy angled nature and broken crags of the Lakeland fells make them ideal for this kind of elementary rock climbing.

LEFT: Mark Januszewski on the 'crux' pitch of Cam Crag Ridge, Langstrath, near Borrowdale: one of the best scrambles in Lakeland. The technical rock climbing venue of Sergeant Crag Slabs can be seen on the opposite side.

ABOVE: David Halsted and Dave Birkett relaxing at the base of Dove Crag; Mark Januszewski on Sharp Edge, another fine scramble on Blencathra (referred to more commonly as Saddleback by locals); Dove Crag, home to steep climbing and the 'Priest Hole' cave, Dovedale.

OVERLEAF: Probably the most popular scramble in the Lake District, Striding Edge on Helvellyn. Main shot taken on a winter evening. INSERTS: The author and friends on Striding Edge in summer, followed by a rest in the summit shelter of Helvellyn.

ABOVE: Jim Birkett, circa 1940, climbs *Arrowhead Ridge* on the Napes Crag (the climb is a venerable 'Very Difficult' route and lies to the left of the Napes Needle). Grandson Dave Birkett makes the first repeat ascent of *Breathless*, (E8) on Tophet Wall, Napes Crag, touted at the time (2004) as 'the world's hardest traditional route'. The contrast between these two routes demonstrates the evolution of rock climbing over the past century from easy angled slabs to unrelentingly overhanging rock. *Photos courtesy of Bill Birkett photo library*.

RIGHT: Great Gable with a dusting of snow, as seen from Lingmell. Napes Crag in full view including the famous Napes Needle for the keen eye. The overhanging Tophet Wall lies in the steep shadow at the very right hand side of the crag.

PREVIOUS SPREAD: A wild day at Grisedale Tarn en route for fell walkers' favourite, Fairfield.

Whichever mountain craft you choose to pursue, whether it be dangerous, extreme climbs or gentle strolls in the hills, the underlying motive is universal: enjoyment of physical activity within the unique ambience of the Lakeland fells.

ABOVE: Smouldering summits as seen from the top of Great Gable. (Sketch of this image on pages 170-71.)

Alpine Window

The English Alps, ice and white magic

PREVIOUS SPREAD: Dave Birkett on his grandfather's winter classic *Inaccessible Gully*, Dove Crag; 360-degree view of a frozen Stickle Tarn and Pavey Ark.

ABOVE: Winter snow showers pass east of 'The Band', the classic approach to Bowfell. The south-facing Langdale Pikes are easily stripped of snow whereas the north side of Pike o'Blisco remains well covered.

Alpine Window

Wintry weather has a dramatic transformative effect on the Lakeland fells. Even the most modest peak can appear twice as high once snow has taken grip of its upper reaches. The change is not just visual, but also physical; snow and ice require a totally new set of skills to negotiate the fells safely. What would normally be an easy hike or scramble becomes a potentially dangerous outing requiring the use of crampons and ice axes. Despite modern equipment, the challenge remains; there are nearly always casualties during a cold snap thanks to hikers being surprised by full winter conditions and a simple slip on an exposed piece of ice can mean the difference between life and death.

If anything, Lakeland fell-goers today are likely to be less prepared for the challenge of winter than their older peers. The season is becoming warmer and less snowy. Pictures from guidebooks only a couple of decades old boast of heavy snow falls and ice formations seldom seen in recent years. Winter climbers active in the past reminisce fondly how the winter season could be at least three or four months long with fell tops frequently snow covered from December to March. Until the 1970s, it was not uncommon for small patches of snow to survive through a summer in a few high, sheltered, north-facing corries and hollows, something unseen for over a generation now.

Even in my mere ten years of climbing and photographing in Lakeland the experience has shifted quite dramatically. Lots of rain, wind, grey skies and mildness are my prevailing memories of winter in the Lakes. Some seasons now

pass where the temperatures are so warm and snowfall so elusive that no actual winter climbing is possible at all. That said, traditional winter conditions do still arrive in the Lakes, albeit with greater unpredictability, and when they do it is all the more reason to marvel and cherish such an experience while we still can. The keen winter climber must ring in sick, cancel birthdays and abandon families for the chance to grasp the alpine window of opportunity. Photographers and sightseers must also head to the hills and marvel at the arctic makeover. Suddenly the Lake District mountain landscape comes to the fore. The English Alps are back, if only for a short period.

This, then, is my favourite time for photography, when winter snows transform Lakeland briefly into a raw, wilder state. In addition to the myriad ice and snow formations that create intriguing new shapes from the landscape, cold temperatures bring sharper light. I therefore have to remain optimistic that more good winters will still occur and that this chapter won't have to be re-titled 'Remember The Ice Age?' in 20 years' time.

RIGHT TOP: Gaz Howell ambles up an easy gully on Scafell Pike's main crag in superb winter conditions (Christmas 1999). RIGHT BOTTOM: Dave Birkett with fellow Langdale resident Mark 'Ed' Edwards makes the first and only winter ascent of *Gimmer Crack* in blizzard conditions (March 2006, Grade XII). *Photo Mark Edwards.*

Over a hundred years ago, in the days of genuinely prolonged Lakeland winters, the early climbers – with their Alpine proclivities – displayed remarkably advanced skills on snow and ice. Astonishingly, the world's first Grade 5 ice climb did not occur in the Alps, or even in Scotland, but in England, when a team led by the famous chemist and climber Norman Collie ascended *Steep Gill* on Scafell in 1891 – an ascent that was about half a century ahead of its time. During the 1930s, working-class climbers such as Jim Birkett and Sid and Jammy Cross of Kendal also quietly pushed standards with futuristic ascents of hard ice and 'mixed' routes, such as *Inaccessible Gully* in Dovedale, *Chock Gully* on Dollywaggon Pike and Bowfell Buttress. These routes – all Grade 4 or 5 climbs and still considered very respectable challenges – were all the more impressive given the equipment of the day. Hand and footholds were chipped with axes in the snow and ice – an incredibly strenuous form of climbing compared to today when two ice tools are used for direct traction. The climbers also operated within very small margins of safety given the lack of protection devices available to them. Equipment had scarcely changed from that employed before the Great War. The few advances tended to be personal innovations. Climbers manufactured much of their own kit, such as waterproof overmitts constructed from the rubberised canvas used in soft-top cars. Sid Cross, being a

shoemaker by trade and employed by K's in Kendal, was adept at adapting clothing for winter climbing. Old waxed jackets cast-off from wealthier folk were re-proofed, cut down to waist level, and served as robust waterproofs. Underneath the trousers, pyjama bottoms were worn, much as thermal leggings are today. On their feet were nailed boots – crampons were spurned in Lakeland until after the Second World War.

ABOVE LEFT: Rock climbing master Jim Birkett makes a rare venture into winter climbing, although he made the first ascent of one of the best winter climbs in the Lakes with *Inaccessible Gully* on Dove Crag, circa 1940. It was the ascent of this route that led him to dismiss winter climbing as 'cold and nasty'. The route was all the more impressive as Jim climbed it wearing 'tricounis' (a form of metal nail hammered into the boot) and sporting an unwieldy long-handled ice-axe.

ABOVE CENTRE: Mark 'Ed' Edwards keeping warm belaying at the base of Scafell's East Buttress while Dave Birkett battles up another new, desperately hard, winter climb.

ABOVE RIGHT: Plumb vertical icicles hanging from Scafell's East Buttress indicate its steepness.

A rare sight: a frozen Stickle Tarn and Pavey Ark in an icy grip. Thanks to its south-facing aspect and its lowly altitude of 570m, it takes a prolonged cold spell to freeze the free-flowing damp gullies of the cliffs into a solid state. A thaw was forecast for the following day and temperatures were already rising when we visited this transient piece of the arctic. Colin Wells leads the way up Little Gully in good condition.

Overleaf: Tucked away out of sight in the hanging valley of Comb Gill above Borrowdale lies one of Lakeland's most aesthetic – and fleeting – climbs. In summer, *Raven Crag Gully* is a crypt-like defile of water-trickled rocks and mossy ledges culminating in a cliff-top ampitheatre, which can only be escaped by means of a soaking, soaring slab. When caught in the wintery maw of a hard frost however, the gully is transformed: the final slab becomes a rippling cascade frozen in mid-flight. Raven Crag rarely provides the Lakeland climber with such a glittering prize, but when it does, the investment of patience, often over many long years, feels repaid many times over.

Great End marks the north-east termination of the Scafell range. Due to its altitude (720m) and north-easterly aspect, winter climbing conditions often persist stubbornly here longer than anywhere else in the Lake District. This fact, together with its abundance of moderate and easier gully lines, ensure it is one of Lakeland's most popular winter climbing venues.

ABOVE FROM THE TOP: The outlook from *Central Gully* on Great End; A busy day on *Central Gully, Left Hand* (Grade 3), Great End; Dave Halsted and Gaz Howell head for the summit after an ascent of *Central Gully, Great End.*

117

OVERLEAF: A view from almost the same point on the same day looking south. Pillar is the mountain to the
right, while the Scafell range and Great Gable are on the left.

An imperious Pillar Rock caught in winter shadow rises above a spectacular cloud inversion flowing in from the coast to smother Buttermere and Borrowdale, while Helvellyn and its satellites lie in another world bathed by sunshine. A scene which epitomises the transformative effect of winter on the landscape.

ABOVE TOP: Pillar Rock looms threateningly on the approach from the east.
ABOVE: Looking west from Pillar's sublime summit with the Isle of Man just visible on the right horizon.

OVERLEAF: I had endured an epic journey to reach the summit of Pillar. A three-hour drive to Buttermere was followed by a 45-minute thrash on a mountain bike to the mountain's base. However, I had completely misjudged the conditions; expecting a thaw, I had gambled that the snow would be soft enough to kick steps all the way to the top. (With all my heavy camera equipment I was looking for an excuse to leave the crampons and axes behind.) As I climbed higher, the snow became firmer and icier. I was driven on however, by the fact that the light was getting better all the time and a cloud inversion was developing. Eventually I found myself scrabbling up bullet-hard névé with bare hands and approach shoes (don't tell my mum). Anyway, apart from having to reverse it all in the dark, things worked out okay.

PREVIOUS SPREAD: Looking north from Pillar to the High Stile range, Derwent Fells and Skiddaw beyond. (Sketch of this image on page 168.)

LEFT: Looking south from Pillar's summit to the Scafell range. I hung around until the short winter daylight faded completely, reluctant to leave the otherworldly ambience created by the tranquil dusk light. It seemed more like Alaska or northern Greenland. Wherever you looked the arctic beauty was extraordinarily powerful. (Sketch of this image on page 169.)

One of the most beautiful of phenomena sought by winter climbers occurs when rocks and cliffs become coated in rime and hoar frost. This requires a mixture of both cold and humid conditions: a combination that seems to be becoming rarer. If you want to see or climb it, you must act fast.

ABOVE: En route for Scafell looking up to Pikes Crag from Hollow Stones as the morning sun begins to strip the rock of its transient white coating.

ABOVE TOP: Scafell Pike Crag shows the immediate effects of the sun, as seen from Mickledore. ABOVE RIGHT: Scafell Crag thinly coated with hoar frost; Boulders on top of Scafell rimed after being blasted by icy winds.

OVERLEAF: Scafell Pike and Scafell under a dusting of snow, seen from the slopes of Lingmell.

ABOVE: Looking down Kirkstone Pass over Brother's Water to Place Fell, the traditional route to the Eastern Fells. RIGHT: From the summit of Place Fell (675m) looking north to Blencathra/Saddleback – the classic alpine ridge of Sharp Edge is clearly defined on the right of its summit.

*'One or two fells have Celtic names, such as Helvellyn and Blencathra, while quite
a number of the rivers still keep on murmuring in Welsh, including the Eden,
the Derwent, the Esk and the Leven. But in the villages, the farms, and in the
work and speech of the people, the old Celtic tongue is almost entirely forgotten.'*

Norman Nicholson

Sometimes it's interesting to avoid the popular and spectacular mountains and find one you've never heard of on the map or one you spot driving by and just head up it without knowing its name, height or what the top may be like.

<small>ABOVE:</small> Valerie Le Clerc stands on the open aspect of Place Fell with the far eastern fells of Ill Bell, High Street, Thornthwaite Beacon and Red Screes beyond. (Sketch of this image on page 172.)

ABOVE: The Helvellyn Range as seen from Fairfield on a wild day. The strength of the wind made it almost impossible to set up a tripod.

OVERLEAF: The eastern corries running from below Helvellyn's summit through Nethermost Pike to Dollywaggon Pike is one of the most reliable and popular winter climbing arenas in the Lake District, with many easy routes. Scotland is just in view on the northern horizon, across the Solway Firth.

'Thou hast clomb aloft, and gazed
From the watch-towers of Helvellyn;
Awed, delighted, and amazed!'

William Wordsworth

LEFT: A partly-frozen Grizedale Tarn; a good indicator that winter climbs on Helvellyn will be in condition.

ABOVE: Descending from Dollywaggon Pike; spectacular shafts of sun spotlight the western fells.

The sprawling Helvellyn massif encompasses the third highest peak in the Lake District and provides a focus for winter climbing. Helvellyn's summit itself is just hidden by the clouds. Striding Edge and Nethermost Cove lie to the left and Catstye Cam to the right. Taken from the lower slopes of Place Fell above Ullswater.

The perennially popular Striding Edge, Helvellyn's alpine arête.

RIGHT: Two figures can be spotted on the far right apex of the ridge.

OVERLEAF: Red Tarn Cove and a frozen Red Tarn under winter moonlight. When I arrived to take this picture it was completely dark and since the wind had covered the tarn in spindrift I accidentally walked out onto the tarn before I realised I was on the ice.

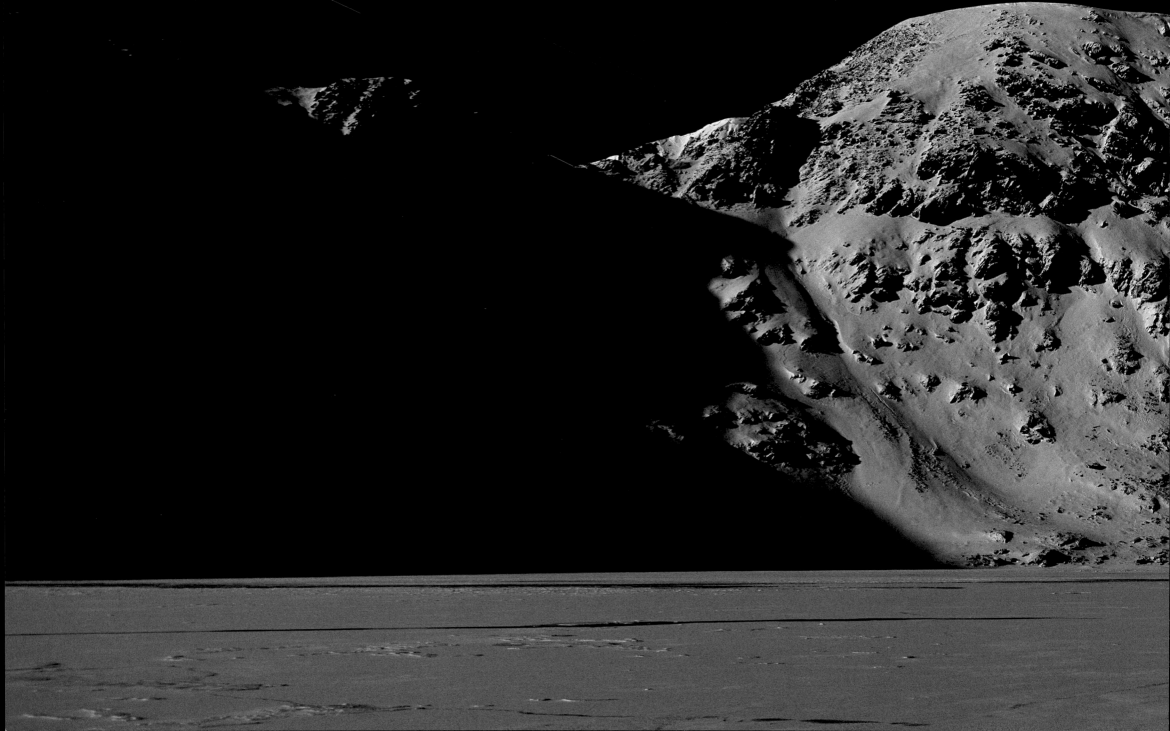

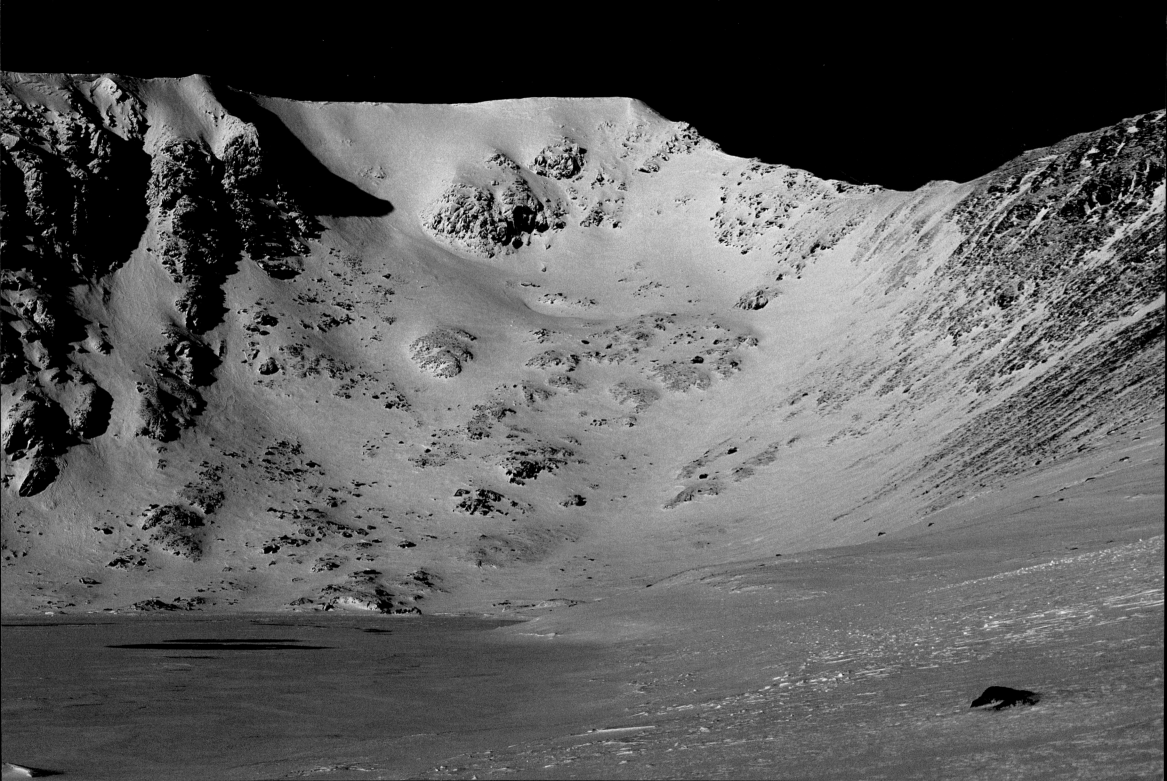

Grisedale Tarn as seen on the descent from Dollywaggon Pike. Lake Windermere and Morecambe Bay glisten distantly beyond the snowy mountains.

Heavy snows transform Dovedale into an alpine valley.

LEFT: *Inaccessible Gully* follows the hanging rift, dropping from the brooding shadowed black mass of Dove Crag on the left. The thin pencil of ice comprising another classic but infrequently forming winter route, *Black Crag Icefall*, can just be discerned splitting the sunny crag on the right.

ABOVE: Dave Birkett on his grandfather's classic winter climb, *Inaccessible Gully*, Dove Crag, Dovedale. Dave had a transcendental experience when climbing this route by moonlight one evening after work. He was surprised to find the climbing remarkably easy, almost as if he was 'floating up the route', whereas his partner found it desperately hard. It came as a revelation to Dave the next day when he learned that the route had originally been pioneered by his grandfather, Jim, nearly seventy years before. The feeling of relaxed calm Dave had experienced suddenly began to make sense: 'He was with me', he explained.

Photographic Notes

Camera, action, light

Lightweight tripod and Fuji 617 panoramic camera set up on Pillar's summit after a
desperate sprint and climb to the top as the light faded.

I'm often asked how to take good landscape photographs. Admittedly it can be difficult, but not for the reasons you might think. When out in the field, I'm usually on my own, sometimes with my wife, sometimes with a good friend, but most of the time it's just me. As I'm going up, everybody else is coming down, and when I'm coming down, everybody else is going up. This gives you a massive hint as to the secret of landscape photography: timing. You need to be out there during the first and last hour of the day and, if you want good mountain landscapes, this means plenty of walking in the dark, probably on your own. Whilst you can second guess the conditions from weather forecasts and synoptic charts to some extent, you just need to get out as much as you can, at these 'right times'. 'Get out more and take fewer photographs', is a photographic truism, meaning, essentially, observe more, increase your chances of being in the right place at the right time and concentrate on the quality of image, rather than quantity. All very well, but when you are juggling family and business with photography it gets complicated, especially if you don't live 'on location'. The Lake District is a good hour's drive from my house in Lancashire which meant more like two to three hours to reach the fells and hike into position. I don't consider the technical elements of photography to be particularly complicated; there's not that much to remember and once you're in the swing of it you can do it with your eyes shut (although it's nearly always better to keep them open). Set the camera up on a tripod, compose your shot, check the horizon is level (spirit level in tripod), check exposure with light meter, set camera accordingly (is it a 90mm lens with a centre spot grad filter? If so push down one stop) keep aperture under F22 for corner to corner sharpness, check focus, take several exposures bracketing the shot as experience dictates.

Now, that might sound like a lot, but it's not really. How hard can anything be that can be explained in one long ungrammatical sentence? No, what is difficult about landscape photography is being 'in the right place at the right time'. Decisions need to be made quickly. Conditions may change rapidly, so do you keep heading for your original destination which is now not looking so great – or gamble and head for somewhere else? Uncertainty provides the excitement. You may find yourself pushing on to a summit or vantage point exhausted, legs pumping, sweat flooding through your clothes, hoping for something special when you get there. It never ceases to amaze me, no matter how well planned any particular shot has been, that I can just miss out on the decisive moment by a matter of minutes or even seconds, or how on other occasions I just get the shot by the skin of my teeth. Something else to bear in mind is that the large format panoramic photography on display in this book takes a lot more time to set up and capture than a point-and-shoot 35mm SLR or digital camera. Not only does everything need to be mounted on a tripod but you cannot see what you have taken until a few days later when the films are processed. This means the capturing of spontaneous conditions is tricky, but makes it all the more rewarding when you get it right.

PAGES 154–155: No greater artist than nature, snow waves on Kentmere Pike; The author behind the viewfinder; 360-degree view from Esk Hause at sunrise; a serendipitous shot – I intended to be on Esk Pike by this time.

PREVIOUS SPREAD: Wrynose Pass, the quickest way to make easy work of a good vantage point.

LEFT: Valerie Le Clerc, a master at waiting around in the cold; the author and photographer trying to keep his digits warm in order to change another roll of film in bitter conditions on Helvellyn.

There's an endless debate over the influence of computers in modern photography, with many dismissing the use of photo editing software as 'cheating'. I take the view that the photographer should embrace the digital revolution. Editing software can be regarded as a digital darkroom, just another tool used to accomplish a certain end, as much as a tripod, lens or film might be. As Ansel Adams said: 'there are no rules for good photographs, there are only good photographs.'

Once the preserve of specialist photographers, the panoramic format has become increasingly popular in the last few years thanks to the availability of software which enables the seamless stitching of several images to create a panoramic effect. I too used this technique during my earliest attempts to achieve the desired all-encompassing landscapes – except this was before sophisticated stitching software had evolved. I'd take about 18 shots for a 360-degree image and then spend up to eight hours putting it together. Whilst it was a good learning experience, I soon got tired of the mammoth computer editing sessions and was never fully satisfied with the results.

The Roundshot camera used for the panoramas in this book uses a very different method. It has a cylindrical film plate that rotates as the image is captured, resulting in uninterrupted and sometimes mind-boggling exposures. This camera was used to capture all the 360-degree scenes and a lot of the standard panoramic images. It's a little more complex to set up and use, isn't great in bad weather (as there's so much circuitry) plus it can't capture a smooth image in strong winds and, oh, it weighs a whopping 7kg (without a lens). However, when it does work the results are unique. One of the main advantages of the Roundshot is that it can vary exposure as it rotates, allowing, for example, for the soft light of the evening sun and the brightness of the sun itself to be captured in the same shot. It's also possible to take shots directly into the sun without the normal amount of lens flare by using a special slit filter attachment. The resulting transparency (which measures 22cm x 6cm for a 360-degree image) is then scanned on a high quality scanner and the digital image is 're-touched' – in most cases simply to match the original transparency as closely as possible. Occasionally some 'heavier' editing is necessary where I can see potential in an image but due to the technical nature of the shoot or my own incompetence I didn't quite get it right. Most commonly, this involves balancing the exposure, sometimes referred to as HDR imaging. It's an interesting technique but care must be taken as the image can easily take on an artificial look more akin to a painting than a photograph.

No lens filters were used for the photographs in this book. The Fuji Velvia film used is largely responsible for the saturated colour rendition. Provia 100 and 400ASA film was used for many of the winter and moonlight shots.

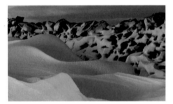

RIGHT TOP: The Roundshot Super 220VR camera; As well as a panoramic camera I always carry a smaller medium format camera (Mamiya 645). This is much better for capturing close-up texture.

BELOW: The author appears twice in the same shot of Keswick town square, an image which displays the rotational qualities of the Roundshot camera to full effect.

Capturing the decisive moment is much easier with a standard 35mm SLR camera.

FAR RIGHT: The author and friends go mad in the summertime, Wasdale.

NEAR RIGHT: Contrasting lifestyles: David Halsted and Dave Birkett seeing the funny side at Dove Crag.

Ultimately, what makes a good image isn't really down to big cameras or high quality lenses: it's desire. I started this project almost half a decade ago and now I am finally writing the last words. I make no claim that this book forms any sort of definitive collection of pictures representing the Lake District landscape – I personally don't feel 'definitive' exists. (I've already had ideas for several more shots since concluding my image gathering – it's a never-ending creative process that seems to increase proportionately to the energy you put into it.) This book merely displays the fruits of my labour during a particular time-frame and owes much to some good fortune with rare weather conditions. I was also lucky enough not to be under any deadline pressure so I could wait until I felt I had garnered sufficiently strong images to match the ambition of my original concept. I hope the viewer shares my feeling that it was time well spent.

Many of the panoramic images were captured with the 'benchmark' equipment: the Fuji GX617 (no longer in production) using a 90mm and 300mm lens. The robust build and lack of electronics make this camera more suitable for the mountain environment than some others.

RIGHT: The Langdale Pikes photographed while en route for Crinkle Crags, the author's shadow in shot.

Peaks in Sketch

Names, heights and points of interest

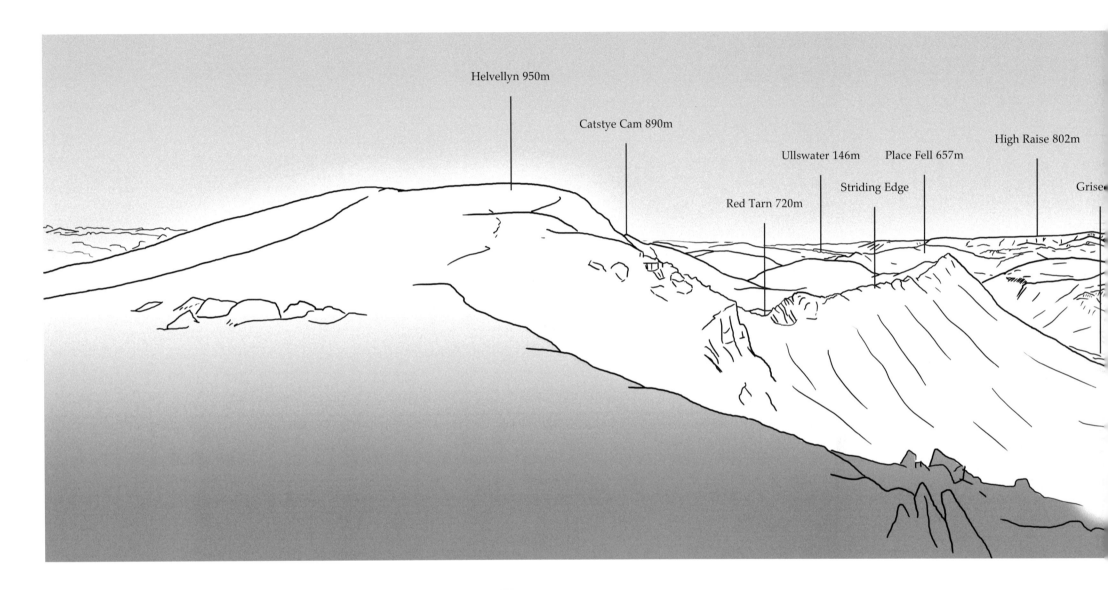

Helvellyn 950m

Catstye Cam 890m

High Raise 802m

Ullswater 146m

Place Fell 657m

Striding Edge

Grise

Red Tarn 720m

360-degree view from just below Helvellyn's summit (910m).
Original photograph on pages 58–59.

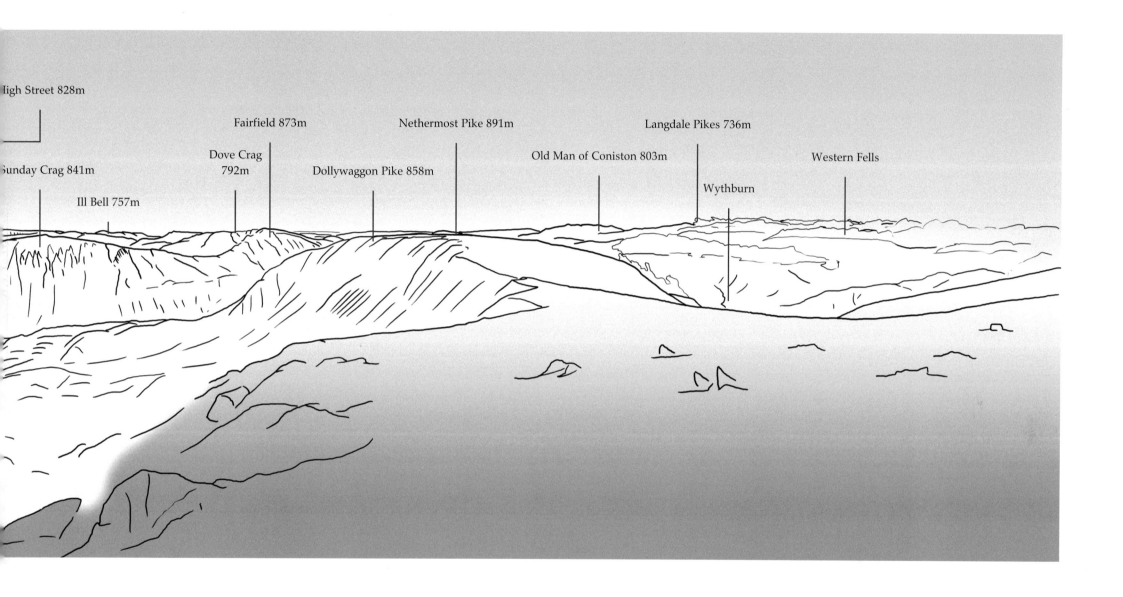

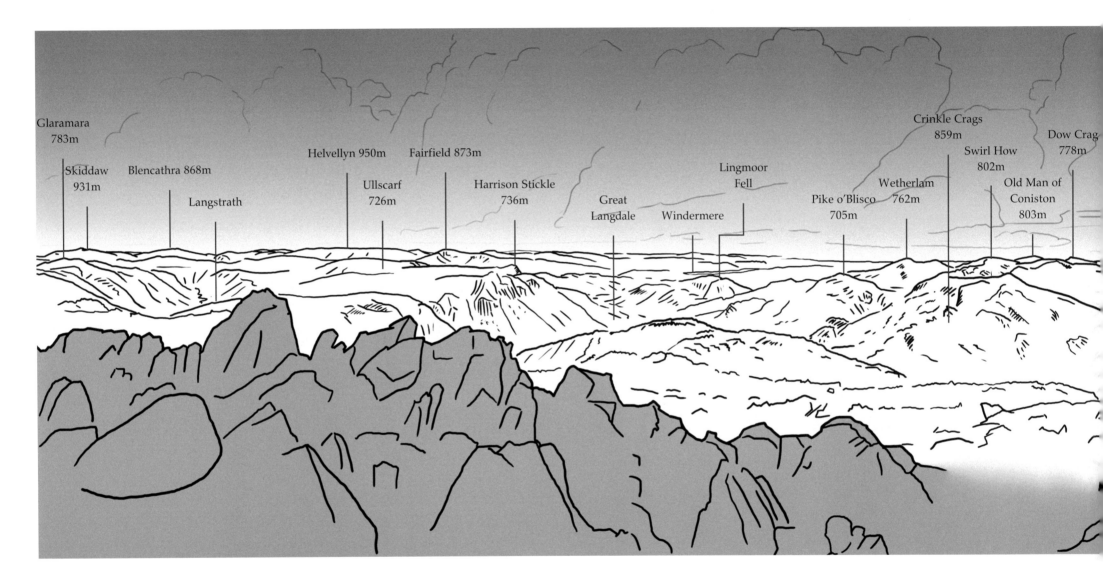

Glaramara
783m

Skiddaw
931m

Blencathra 868m

Langstrath

Helvellyn 950m

Ullscarf
726m

Fairfield 873m

Harrison Stickle
736m

Great
Langdale

Windermere

Lingmoor
Fell

Pike o'Blisco
705m

Wetherlam
762m

Crinkle Crags
859m

Swirl How
802m

Old Man of
Coniston
803m

Dow Crag
778m

360-degree panorama from Bowfell's summit (902m).
Original photograph on pages 16–17.

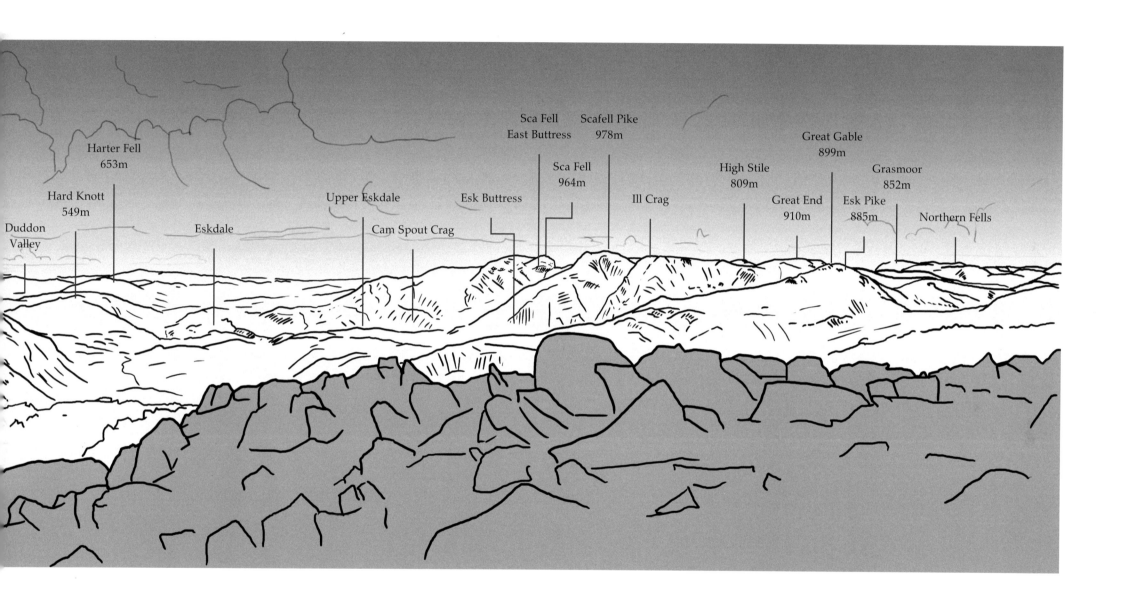

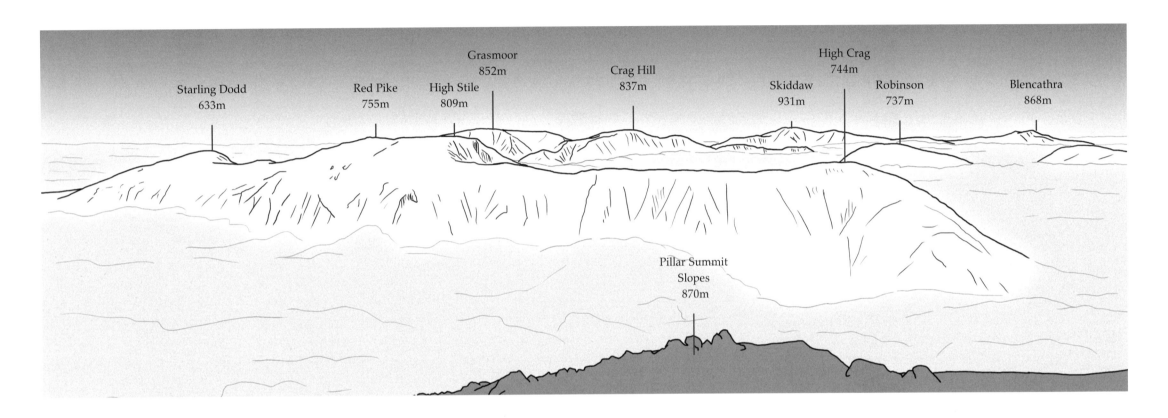

Starling Dodd
633m

Red Pike
755m

High Stile
809m

Grasmoor
852m

Crag Hill
837m

Skiddaw
931m

High Crag
744m

Robinson
737m

Blencathra
868m

Pillar Summit
Slopes
870m

High Stile range from Pillar.
Original photograph on pages 124–125.

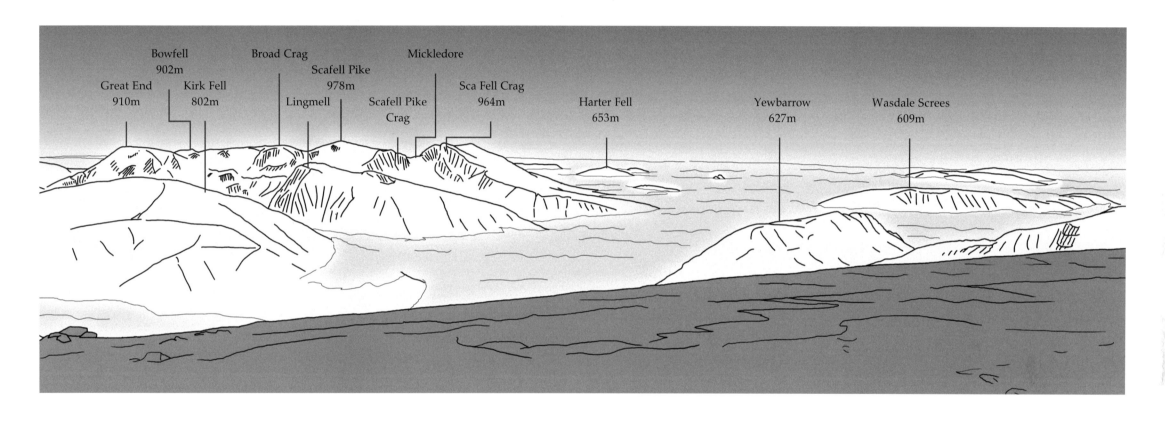

Great End
910m

Bowfell
902m

Kirk Fell
802m

Broad Crag

Scafell Pike
978m

Lingmell

Scafell Pike
Crag

Mickledore

Sca Fell Crag
964m

Harter Fell
653m

Yewbarrow
627m

Wasdale Screes
609m

Scafell range from Pillar (892m).
Original photograph on pages 126–127.

169

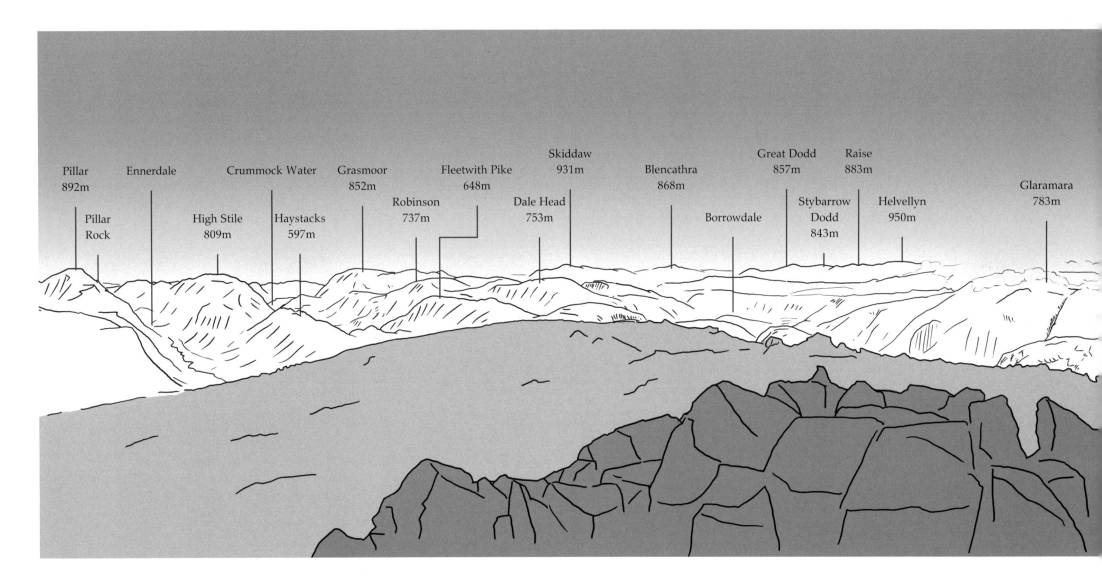

Pillar
892m

Pillar
Rock

Ennerdale

High Stile
809m

Crummock Water

Haystacks
597m

Grasmoor
852m

Robinson
737m

Fleetwith Pike
648m

Skiddaw
931m

Dale Head
753m

Blencathra
868m

Borrowdale

Great Dodd
857m

Stybarrow
Dodd
843m

Raise
883m

Helvellyn
950m

Glaramara
783m

360-degree view from Great Gable's summit (899m).
Original photograph on pages 104–105.

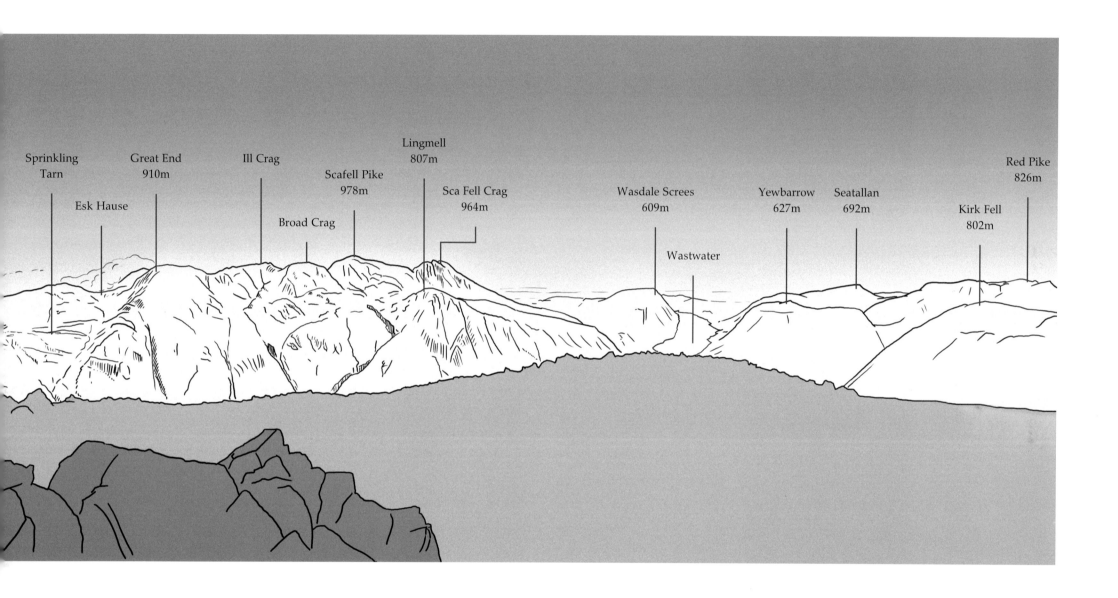

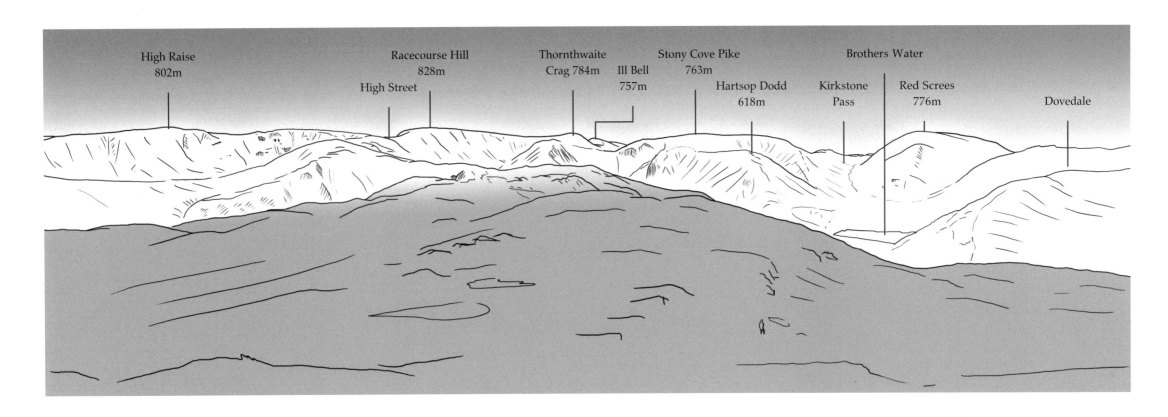

High Raise
802m

Racecourse Hill
828m

High Street

Thornthwaite
Crag 784m

Ill Bell
757m

Stony Cove Pike
763m

Hartsop Dodd
618m

Brothers Water

Kirkstone
Pass

Red Screes
776m

Dovedale

Eastern Fells from Place Fell (657m).
Original photograph on page 136.

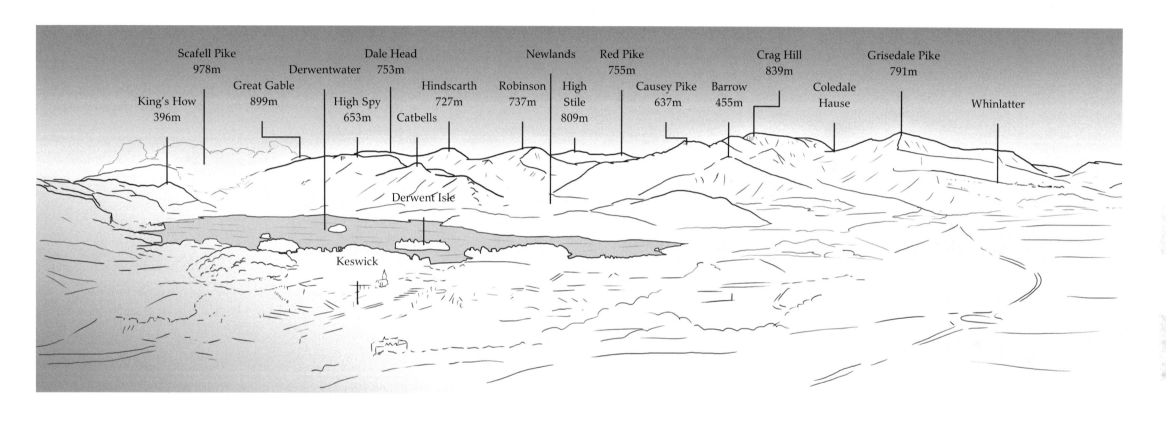

King's How
396m

Scafell Pike
978m

Great Gable
899m

Derwentwater

High Spy
653m

Dale Head
753m

Catbells

Hindscarth
727m

Derwent Isle

Keswick

Robinson
737m

Newlands

High
Stile
809m

Red Pike
755m

Causey Pike
637m

Barrow
455m

Crag Hill
839m

Coledale
Hause

Grisedale Pike
791m

Whinlatter

Keswick and the Northern Fells as seen from Latrigg.
Original photograph on pages 46–47.

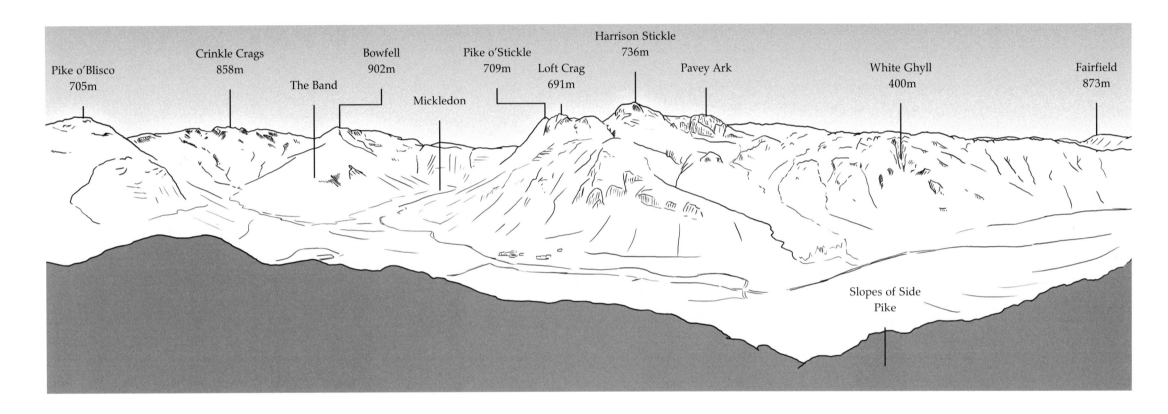

Pike o'Blisco
705m

Crinkle Crags
858m

The Band

Bowfell
902m

Mickledon

Pike o'Stickle
709m

Loft Crag
691m

Harrison Stickle
736m

Pavey Ark

White Ghyll
400m

Fairfield
873m

Slopes of Side
Pike

Langdale Pikes from Side Pike.
Original photograph on pages 50–51.

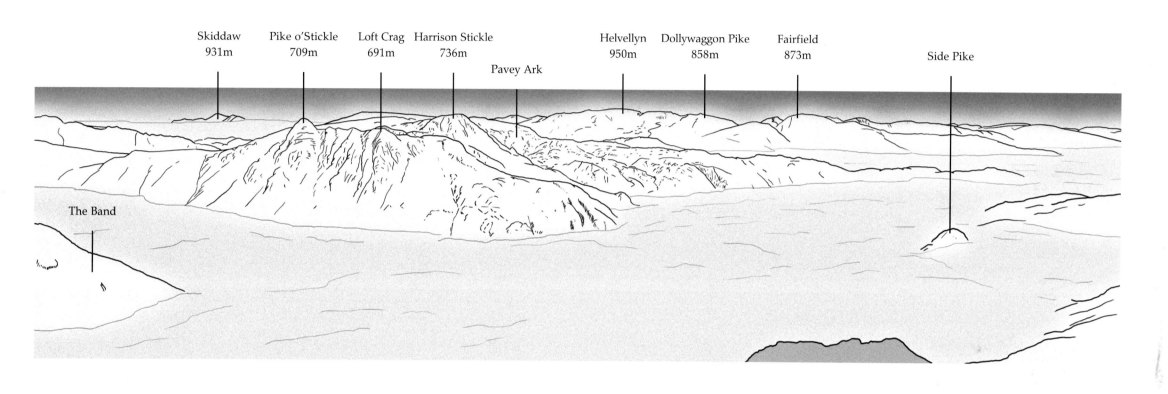

Skiddaw
931m

Pike o'Stickle
709m

Loft Crag
691m

Harrison Stickle
736m

Pavey Ark

Helvellyn
950m

Dollywaggon Pike
858m

Fairfield
873m

Side Pike

The Band

Langdale Pikes from Pike o'Blisco (705m).
Original photograph on pages 22–23.

The Lake District might well be the most written-about piece of landscape in the world. From the Romantic poets to Stuart Maconie, there has been a torrent of words describing, praising, celebrating – and occasionally lambasting – this most rugged of England's corners. Luckily, not all are essential reading. Here, I pick those books which have stood the test of time and which will enable the curious to reach a deeper understanding of the themes behind this book.

New Perspectives

Enclosure, **Andy Goldsworthy. Thames & Hudson (2007)**
Internationally renowned artist Andy Goldsworthy often uses the Lake District as the setting for his sculptures that work with the grain of the landscape. This book features astonishing Cumbrian slate works and balanced stones embedded in walls, along with sixteen sheepfolds reconstructed by the master landscape interpreter.

Norman Nicholson: Collected Poems, **edited by Neil Curry. Faber & Faber (1998)**
Millom-born poet Nicholson frequently took his home county as his subject but he was just as likely to write about decaying ironworks as drystone walls. A poet for sure, but certainly not in the romantic tradition, and with an insider's eye that understood the underlying complexity behind the Lake District landscape better than any off-comer.

Hidden Landscape

The Lake District: A Landscape History, **W.H. Pearsall and W. Pennington. Collins New Naturalist (1974)**
A magnificent synthesis of all the natural and human forces that have shaped the Lakeland landscape by two of British Ecology's greatest scientists. Unlikely to be surpassed.

Cumbria, **Roy Millward and Adrian Robinson. Macmillan (1972)**
Millward and Robinson were professional geographers whose thorough but accessible interpretations of landscape evolution have rarely been bettered.

The Geomorphology of the Lake District: A Field Guide, **edited by John Boardman. Environmental Change Unit, Oxford University (1997)**
An indispensable guide to the often-surprising geographical factors behind the modern landscape.

The Stone Circles of Cumbria, **John Waterhouse. Phillimore (1985)**
An excellent guide to (and explanation of) the fascinating prehistoric monuments that form such a defining aspect of the district's character.

Interpreting the Axe Trade, **Richard Bradley & Mark Edmonds. Cambridge University Press (1993)**
A masterful explanation of the results from recent excavations at the Langdale stone axe factories along with an overview of the prehistoric axe trade by one of Britain's most insightful archaeologists.

The Lowland Wetlands of Cumbria, **David Hodgkinson et al. Lancaster Imprints (2000)**
Although ostensibly about the peatlands of the district, this book also includes an up-to-date synthesis of the archaeology and environmental history of the area.

Mountain Craft

The First Tigers/Century on the Crags/Camera on the Crags, **Alan Hankinson. Dent (1972/1988); Cambridge (1990)**
The former ITN news editor and historian Alan Hankinson wrote the definitive history of the origins of rock climbing in these three excellent and thoroughly readable volumes, the last of which concentrates on the photograhic legacy of the Abraham brothers.

The Coniston Tigers, **Harry Griffin. Sigma Press (1999)**
Journalist Harry Griffin was an active rock climber from the 1930s until the 70s and famous as the Guardian's Lakeland country diarist for nearly 40 years. This is an autobiography of sorts which reveals much about the pre-war Lakeland climbing scene. It is also worth reading any of Harry's numerous other books about the Lake District which will give you far more insight into the outdoor scene and environment of the area than the whole of Alfred Wainwright's popular but over-rated walking guides put together.

Feet in the Clouds, **Richard Askwith. Aurum Press (2004)**
A superb account of the agony and the ecstasy behind the most typically Cumbrian of sports: fell-running.

Alpine Window

Lake District Winter Climbs, **edited by Brian Davison and Stephen Reid. FRCC (2006)**
Details every known winter climb in the district, together with some inspiring action shots and an interesting historical section.

Cold Climbs, **Ken Wilson et al. Baton Wicks (2001)**
A celebration of British winter climbing with an extensive section featuring inspirational essays and photographs relating to the Lake District's most famous routes.

Peaks in Sketch

Lakeland Panoramas, **Jim Watson. Cicerone Press (1995)**
An excellent book of sketches focusing on 'Spectacular sights from easy-to-get-to viewpoints'. Very useful for identifying peaks by their physical appearance rather than how they appear according to topography on a map. Also very useful if you want to see some classic Lakeland views and are – to quote the book – 'the aged, the infirm or the just plain lazy'.